THE YOUNG
RUGBY
PLAYER

ANDREW MCQUILLAN

Making contact

Rear tackle

The front row

London • New York • Sydney • Delhi
www.dk.com

A DORLING KINDERSLEY BOOK

www.dk.com

Project Editor Amanda Rayner **Senior Art Editor** Rebecca Johns
Managing Editor Mary Ling
Managing Art Editor Rachael Foster
Photography Steve Gorton **Digital Artwork** Robin Hunter
DTP Designer Almudena Díaz **Picture Research** Liz Moore
Production Lisa Moss and Kenneth McKay

Important safety advice

Only a selection of the many rugby techniques taught are featured in this book. You cannot teach yourself rugby by following the sequences and moves shown on these pages. To learn the correct techniques you must attend training sessions run by a qualified coach.

All clubs will be happy to let you watch a training session before you decide to join. When choosing a club, make sure that it is affiliated to the national rugby union in your country and ask whether they have a coach qualified to instruct players of your age. A list of useful addresses can be found at the back of this book.

Special thanks to Haslemere Junior Rugby Club

First published in Great Britain in 1999
by Dorling Kindersley Limited
9 Henrietta Street, London WC2E 8PS

2 4 6 8 10 9 7 5 3 1

A CIP catalogue record for this book is available from the British Library.

ISBN 0 7513 7220 X

Colour reproduction by Colourscan, Singapore
Printed and bound in Italy by L.E.G.O.

Contents

To all young rugby players

"RUGBY IS A GREAT competitive sport that calls for inspiration and exceptional teamwork. To succeed, you must be physically fit with a positive attitude, both on and off the pitch. I began mini rugby at Bath Rugby Club when I was seven years old and have played for the first team since the age of 19. When I was 23, I won my first cap for England, and since then I've been lucky enough to represent my country in the Rugby World Cup and be selected for the British Lions. Above all, the challenge of playing rugby has taught me how to work well with others to achieve a common goal. For me, nothing can beat the magic of scoring a try – that fantastic feeling when everything comes together after many hard hours of training. Anyone can take part in rugby, whatever their ability. The main thing is to play fair and remember to work as part of a team. I know that you'll enjoy reading this book and hope you get as much fun from rugby as I do!"

Here I am taking a break from training for the Rugby World Cup in South Africa in 1995.

By running through gaps in the opposition defence I can launch powerful attacks for England.

I am getting ready to pass the ball to a team-mate in a British Lions match.

Competition can be tough, as this photograph from a World Cup match against Italy clearly shows.

When sprinting with the ball I always look for support players.

It was brilliant to score a try for England in the 1998 Cook Cup match against Australia. You can see the effort as I touch the ball down over the opposition goal line.

History of rugby

IN THE EARLY 1800s, some versions of football allowed you to catch and kick the ball. When a 16-year-old pupil at Rugby School took this variation a step further by holding the ball and running all the way up the field, he started a whole new game. Gradually, "rugby football" caught on in other schools and as boys left, they set up clubs all over England so that they could continue playing. In the early years the game could be rough, with no limit to the number of players, the size of the pitch, or the time played. Even the shape of the ball varied. In 1871, the Rugby Football Union was formed to establish a clear set of rules and to introduce referees to oversee the games.

William Webb Ellis
This statue at Rugby School shows William Webb Ellis, the schoolboy who first ran with the ball in 1823. This departure from football led to the formal recognition of "rugby football", where players carried the ball to their opponents' end, touching it down for a "try" – the chance to kick the ball between the posts.

Early kit
In the 1830s, players' kit at Rugby School included white trousers, jerseys, and caps. The England team adopted this custom and still plays its matches in white kit, wearing shorts instead of trousers. Caps are no longer worn but the tradition continues. Players are still awarded "caps" when they are selected to play for their country.

Amateur game
Blackheath from southeast London was one of the 20 clubs that founded the Rugby Football Union. The team is pictured in 1895, the year that many other clubs broke away from the Union after a dispute about players' pay and formed a separate game, known as rugby league.

International matches
The first international match was played between England and Scotland in 1871. The International Rugby Board was formed in 1886 to administer the game and now has 90 member countries including China, India, and Brazil. France formed their first team in Le Havre in 1872 and this photograph shows an early match against England in 1923.

The southern hemisphere
The formidable rugby teams of Australia and New Zealand were first formed in the 1860s. England toured against these teams in 1888 and later that year a team of New Zealand Maoris visited Britain. They brought with them their traditional battle challenge, the haka, which the All Blacks still perform before every match they play.

What you will need

THE FIRST THING you need to play rugby is a set of team-mates and the best way to find these is to join a local rugby club. Even more importantly, the club will be able to provide you with a qualified coach to teach you the game, and all the necessary equipment. The basic kit consists of a shirt, shorts, socks, boots, and a mouthguard. You should buy well-fitting boots and strong, comfortable clothing.

Basic kit

Your personal kit should be comfortable, clean, and relatively loose fitting. Shirts are made of cotton or synthetic fabric and are designed to withstand the robust nature of a contact sport. Always tuck your shirt into your shorts to make it more difficult for an opponent to hold on to you.

Quartered shirts, as shown here, are popular with many clubs.

Shirts normally have long sleeves.

Shorts are made of strong cotton with an elasticated waist and a drawstring.

Tie your socks in place with a garter tape to ensure that they stay up.

Your boots must be clean, well fitting, and tightly laced.

Boots

Ideally, you should buy a pair of boots made especially for playing rugby as this will ensure that they have the correct studs. There are various styles of boot. The height over the ankle and instep, the number and height of the studs, and whether the boot has a soft or hard toecap are the main differences.

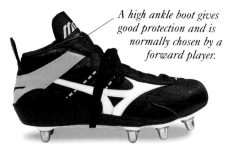

A high ankle boot gives good protection and is normally chosen by a forward player.

A low ankle boot is lighter and a better choice for the faster back players.

Boots have six or eight studs each, screwed into the boot in pairs. These studs are normally made of soft aluminium. They can be 15 mm (0.6 in) or 18 mm (0.7 in) high.

The ball

Rugby balls are egg-shaped, aerodynamic, and made of synthetic material. They come in three different sizes, with smaller ones for younger players. Full-size balls are 280–300 mm (11–12 in) long and weigh 400–440 g (14–16 oz). The shape, size, and textured surface make them easy to grip, even in wet conditions.

The tee

Moulded plastic tees now assist players taking a place kick. The tee, which comes in various heights, enables kickers to angle the ball correctly for the height and distance they wish to achieve.

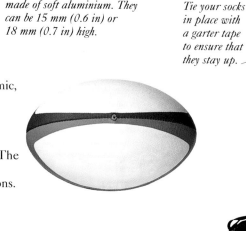

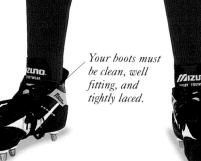

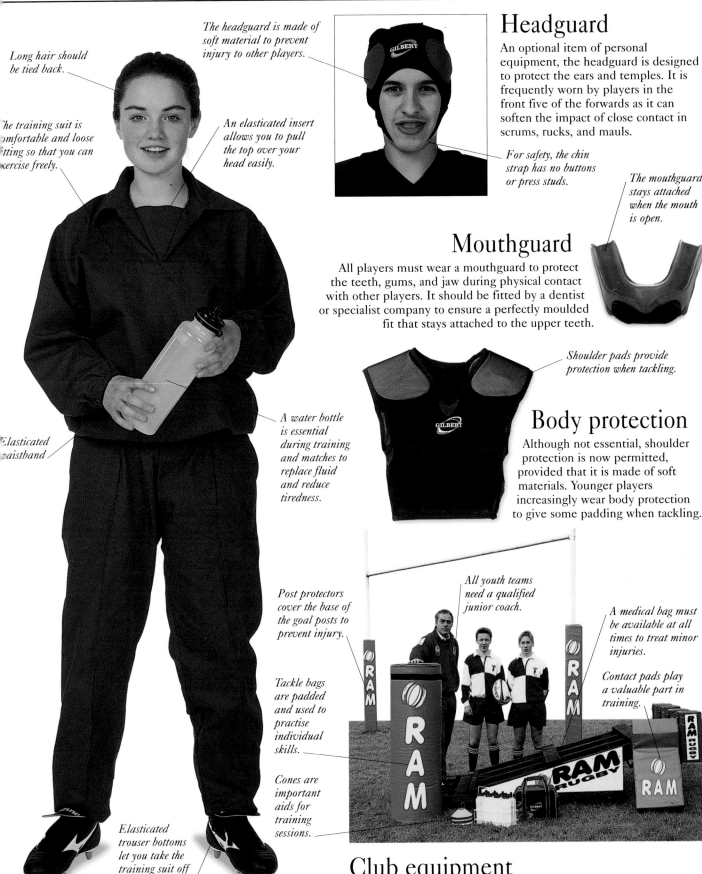

Long hair should be tied back.

The headguard is made of soft material to prevent injury to other players.

The training suit is comfortable and loose fitting so that you can exercise freely.

An elasticated insert allows you to pull the top over your head easily.

Elasticated waistband

Headguard

An optional item of personal equipment, the headguard is designed to protect the ears and temples. It is frequently worn by players in the front five of the forwards as it can soften the impact of close contact in scrums, rucks, and mauls.

For safety, the chin strap has no buttons or press studs.

The mouthguard stays attached when the mouth is open.

Mouthguard

All players must wear a mouthguard to protect the teeth, gums, and jaw during physical contact with other players. It should be fitted by a dentist or specialist company to ensure a perfectly moulded fit that stays attached to the upper teeth.

Shoulder pads provide protection when tackling.

Body protection

Although not essential, shoulder protection is now permitted, provided that it is made of soft materials. Younger players increasingly wear body protection to give some padding when tackling.

A water bottle is essential during training and matches to replace fluid and reduce tiredness.

Post protectors cover the base of the goal posts to prevent injury.

All youth teams need a qualified junior coach.

A medical bag must be available at all times to treat minor injuries.

Tackle bags are padded and used to practise individual skills.

Contact pads play a valuable part in training.

Cones are important aids for training sessions.

Elasticated trouser bottoms let you take the training suit off over your boots.

Training suit

Normally, training suits are made of cotton for strength and warmth. Wear a training suit when you are preparing for a match and put it back on as soon as you stop playing.

Club equipment

The coach needs several training aids, such as tackle bags and contact pads, to train young players effectively and safely. Older players also benefit from access to a scrum machine. For training sessions your club will need different-coloured bibs, cones to mark out training areas, water bottles, and a medical bag. Corner flags and post protectors are essential for all matches.

The pitch and game

Supporters of both teams sit together in the stands.

RUGBY UNION is a challenging contact sport played on a grass pitch by two teams of 15 players. Teams from many countries now take part in international competitions. The game features an oval-shaped ball that can be kicked, carried, and thrown. The pitch is a maximum size of 100 m (109 yd) by 70 m (75 yd), but for players under 12 years old, the length of the game, pitch size, and number of players, are all reduced according to age.

The game

Winning a game

The object of the game is to score more points than the opposition. The referee awards points for tries scored and goals kicked.

Game duration

A game is divided into two halves, each lasting 40 minutes, plus injury time at the end. A coin is tossed at the beginning and the team that wins the toss can choose to kick off or receive the kick.

Attacking and defending

If your team has the ball, you can attack your opponents' goal line. To make progress, you run with the ball, pass it to a team-mate, or kick it up the field. You can only pass sideways or backwards, never forwards. To stop the opponents' forward progress, you can tackle the player with the ball and try to win the ball for your team.

"In touch" and "dead balls"

A ball that hits the ground outside the touchline is out of play, or "in touch". A ball is said to be "dead" when it is not in play.

Line-outs and scrums

If the ball crosses the touchline, play is restarted with a line-out (see pages 32–33). If you accidentally pass the ball forwards, or knock it on, the referee awards a scrum to the other team (see pages 30–31).

Tries and goals

You score a try if you carry the ball over your opponents' goal line and touch it down. This is worth five points and you also get a free kick at goal to gain another two points. You score a goal when you kick the ball over the crossbar. Any player can drop kick a ball over the opponents' crossbar during play and this scores three points.

Offside and penalties

You are in an offside position if you are in front of a team-mate who has the ball or last played the ball. The referee will award a penalty kick or scrum to the other team if you play the ball or obstruct a player while offside.

Advantage law

When a player breaks the laws of the game, but the other team may gain an advantage, the referee will signal that play should continue. If the team does not gain an advantage, the referee will stop play to award a penalty, free kick, or scrum as appropriate.

Twickenham Stadium

Twickenham in West London, UK, has one of the world's great rugby stadiums. It has been the home of English rugby since 1909 and is the headquarters of the Rugby Football Union (RFU), the governing body of rugby in England. The stadium has been completely redeveloped in recent years and now seats more than 75,000 spectators.

Physical contact

Contact sport

Close physical contact is a major part of the game of rugby. With contact comes a potential for injury, so each player must take responsibility for the safety of others.

Respect for others

Young players around the world are taught self-discipline, teamwork, and respect for the referee and the safety of other players.

Safe contact

Learn how to make contact safely from a qualified coach. Make sure that you are warmed up before you play and avoid unnecessary contact, especially with your head. Never tackle a player who is jumping. Always make contact with your shoulder first, especially when tackling. If you are tackled, roll with the impact and move quickly away. Always stop when you hear the referee's whistle.

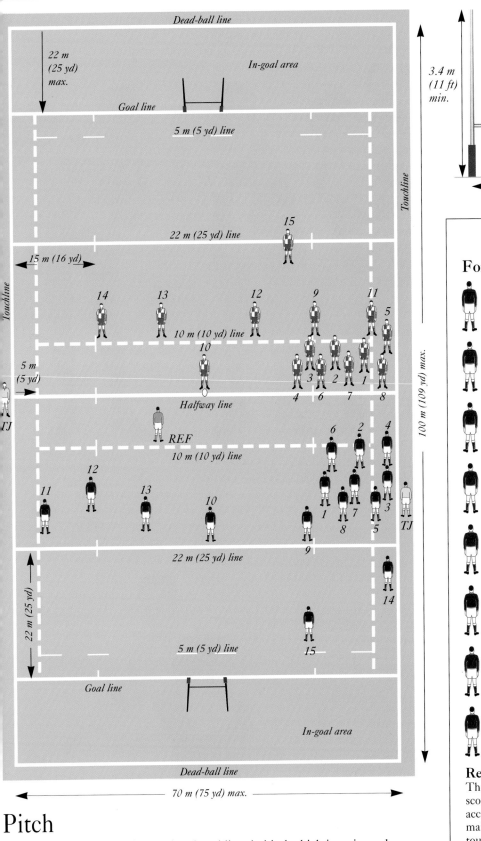

Goal

The uprights of the goal are set 5.6 m (18 ft) apart with a crossbar 3 m (10 ft) high. The posts must be at least 3.4 m (11 ft) high but are usually much taller. Protective padding around the bottom of each post prevents injury to players.

3.4 m (11 ft) min.

3 m (10 ft)

5.6 m (18 ft)

Players' positions

Forwards

Loose-head prop
Front five

Hooker
Front five

Tight-head prop
Front five

Lock
Front five

Lock
Front five

Flanker
Middle five

Flanker
Middle five

No. 8
Middle five

Backs

Scrum-half
Middle five

Fly-half
Middle five

Left wing
Back five

Centre
Back five

Centre
Back five

Right wing
Back five

Full-back
Back five

Referee and touch judges

The referee starts and ends the game, keeps score, and ensures that the game is played according to the laws for both fairness and to maintain the safety of players. There is one touch judge along each side of the pitch who must signal when the ball has gone into touch or when a goal is scored. The referee may overrule their decisions.

 Referee   **Touch judge**

Pitch

At each end of the pitch is a goal and goal line, behind which is an in-goal area where tries can be scored. Lines marked 22 m (25 yd) in front of each goal line and broken lines 10 m (10 yd) each side of the halfway line indicate where players may stand for starts or restarts. Broken lines marked 5 m (5 yd) and 15 m (16 yd) in from each touchline show where players stand for a line-out. Another broken line 5 m (5 yd) in from the goal line indicates the nearest point to the goal line that a scrum may be taken. The diagram shows typical positions for players at the start of a match, with the blue team about to kick off.

Warming up

I T IS ESSENTIAL to warm up thoroughly to avoid injury and prepare mentally for each match or training session. Start with jogging to raise your body temperature, followed by a series of gentle stretches of all your main muscles. The exercises shown here are just a selection of possible warm-up routines. When you have finished training, warm down with some slow stretches.

Roll your arm forwards.

Hold your head straight.

Raise your elbow above your shoulder.

Keep your hips facing forwards.

Shoulder roll

Rugby players must work on their upper bodies to improve strength for tackling and scrummaging. This exercise concentrates on the arms, neck, and shoulders and you should always warm up these areas before a match. Start by rolling your arms and shoulders forwards, then reverse the action by pulling your elbows backwards.

1 Stand with your feet apart, clench your fists, and bend forwards slightly. Roll your arms forwards as if you were swimming the front crawl.

2 Keep your head still and make sure your fists enter the "water" in front of your chest. Try not to let your hips move from side to side as you roll your arms.

3 As you roll each shoulder joint in turn, raise your elbow above your shoulder. Now reverse the exercise by pulling your elbows backwards.

Keep your head up.

Your back must be straight.

Groin stretch

Sit on the ground with your back straight. Bend your legs and place the soles of your feet together. Holding your ankles so that your elbows are inside your knees, push down with your elbows on your inner knees. Be careful not to bounce your knees. Repeat this gently to feel the stretch in your inner thighs.

Press down gently on your knees.

Hold your ankle and slowly pull upwards.

The soles of your feet are together. Pull them gently towards you holding your ankles.

Try not to lean to one side.

Use your free arm to help you balance or rest your hand on a partner's shoulder.

Front thigh stretch

Stand on one leg, hold the free leg behind you by the ankle, and pull it gently up to your bottom. Push your foot down into your hand to increase the stretch. Hold this position for 15–20 seconds, keeping your supporting knee slightly flexed. Repeat several times with each leg.

Calf stretch

Stand with one foot in front of the other with both feet flat on the ground and facing forwards. Keeping your back straight and your head up, gently place your weight onto the front foot and slowly lunge forwards. Repeat for the other leg.

Look straight ahead.

Rest your hands on your hips and keep your hips facing forwards.

Keep your back upright.

Stand with both feet pointing straight ahead.

Make sure that the back heel stays flat on the ground to stretch the calf muscle fully.

Waist stretch

Towards the end of your warm-up, exercise with a rugby ball in your hands to prepare for the coming match. This stretch works the muscles in your waist. Standing back to back with a partner, place your feet shoulder-width apart. Keep your back upright and relax your shoulders. Pass the ball ten times, then reverse the direction.

Twist left and pass the ball smoothly, keeping your back upright.

Twist right and take the ball again.

1 Holding the ball in both hands, twist slowly to the left until you are almost looking behind you and can pass the ball to your partner.

2 Twist gently to the right and take the ball back. Keep the action smooth and consistent throughout.

Back stretch

This is a good general stretching and bending exercise and is more fun if done by two lines of players as a race. You must pass the ball between your legs to the player behind, who passes it over his or her head to the next player. As soon as you have passed the ball, run to the end of the line and wait for it to come to you again.

1 Bend down and pass the ball back through your legs. Your partner should stand far enough back to stretch and take the ball.

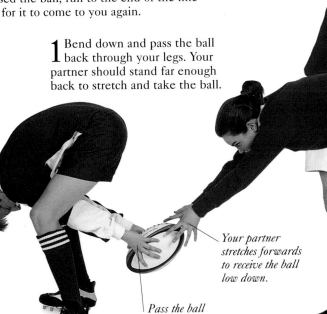

Your partner grips one end of the ball to make it easier for you to receive.

Run behind your partner and take the ball up high.

Your partner stretches backwards to exercise her lower back.

Your partner stretches forwards to receive the ball low down.

Pass the ball back through your legs.

2 Run behind your partner and raise your hands to receive the ball. Your partner stretches up and backwards to pass the ball overhead. Take the ball and get ready to pass it between your legs again.

Your feet should be shoulder-width apart.

Ready to train
As soon as you have warmed up you can start your training session. Put your training suit on to stay warm.

Training sessions

TO PLAY RUGBY properly you need to learn team skills as well as individual techniques. Rugby is a very sociable game because players take part in regular training sessions with their team-mates. As young players mature, the game develops and more team moves are introduced. It is impossible to learn how to play rugby without joining a club that has a qualified coach to guide you during training sessions.

Junior rugby

Rugby can be great fun and involves all the family – children as young as six enjoy the game. Every country has a development scheme that ensures that children only play with others of the same age. In the older age groups, the number of players in each team increases and more of the traditional elements of rugby are added. The aim is to keep the game safe and contact is only introduced when children know how to handle it correctly.

Anyone can play

No matter how large or small, boy or girl, everybody can play rugby. There are 15 players and ten different positions in each team, all with a particular task to perform. Every team needs a mix of large and small players and a balance between strength and speed. As young players develop, the positions in which they play may change, so it is important to learn the skills involved in all positions. For example, a 12-year-old scrum-half may become a prop forward when he is 15.

Always make contact with your shoulder first.

Tackle bags

Determination and technique are the keys to skilful tackling and coaches use tackle bags mainly to teach good technique. The bags are filled with dense foam so that players cannot hurt themselves. Keep your head to one side and hit the tackle bag with your shoulder while placing your arms around it. Think about driving the bag backwards as your coach supports it. Make sure that your head is not under the tackle bag when it falls.

Scrum machines

The scrum is a complicated set piece that requires a lot of practice. Using a scrum machine, the coach can ensure that players are in the right position and working as a unit without the need for another set of players to practise against. To scrum safely and successfully, all players must keep their heads up, their backs straight, and bind tightly together. Never allow your shoulders to fall below your hips, otherwise the scrum is likely to collapse, which can be dangerous to all players.

Training grids

Players can develop various ball-handling skills by forming a training grid. The grid has the advantage of containing players within a small area, which helps them to practise their skills under pressure, forcing them to make quick passes and avoid other players in the area. This photograph shows players from all four corners crossing in the centre of the grid while passing the ball to another player. The coach will provide advice and new ideas on how to improve different types of passes.

Safe practice

Training sessions can be fun. Always listen carefully to your coach, who will teach you the safe and correct way to perform each rugby skill.

Line-out machines

The line-out machine provides an adjustable target for throwing the ball consistently to the desired height and distance. The target represents the line-out jumper's outstretched hands. Good machines also include lower hoops, which provide a target for players practising accurate passing, or higher hoops for kicking practice.

Line-out machines are very useful for hookers practising their throw-in skills.

Never engage (make contact with) the scrum machine until the coach is satisfied with your binding.

Always practise scrummaging with a qualified coach.

RAM RUGBY

Handling and catching

THE MOST IMPORTANT skills in rugby are handling and catching, so you must be able to receive the ball without dropping it. If you fail to catch the ball cleanly and it goes forwards, the referee will penalize you for a knock-on. In addition, the pointed shape of the ball often makes it bounce wildly, so you must feel confident about catching it before it hits the ground. Practise so that catching the ball is second nature to you. Then you will perform much better when you are under pressure during a match.

Keep your eyes fixed on the ball as you prepare to catch it.

Gripping the ball

The most basic skill of all is holding the ball. The shape and texture of the ball help you to get a good grip, which should always be with the fingers and thumbs of both hands. Place one hand on either side of the ball and spread your fingers and thumbs. Hold the ball slightly in front of you as you run so that you are perfectly positioned to pass to either side if necessary.

Handling skills

During a match, the ball may come to you at varying speeds and heights and from different directions. You should practise frequently to get used to the feel and shape of the ball. A figure-of-eight drill will improve your handling skills. When you feel confident, pass the ball faster and try it as you walk forwards.

1 Stand with your feet squarely placed and a little more than shoulder-width apart. Bend forwards at the waist and hold the ball in your left hand in front of your left leg.

2 Push the ball back through your legs with your left hand. Get ready to transfer it carefully to your right hand behind your right leg, taking care not to drop the ball.

3 With your right hand, bring the ball around to the front of your right leg. Then push the ball back through your legs and transfer it to your left hand. Now pass it around your left leg to the front again and repeat the drill.

Making a target

The best place to receive a pass is at chest height. To help your team-mates aim their passes, try to make a clear target. Hold out your hands in front of your chest and half turn to face the ball. As the ball arrives, allow it to hit your target hand first and then close the other hand on to the ball to control it. For example, if the ball comes from the left, it should hit your right hand first.

Spread your fingers to give the maximum contact area for the ball.

Picking up a loose ball

There will often be times in a game when the ball is loose on the ground and you have the chance to pick it up. If you follow the sequence shown here, you should be able to pick the ball off the ground without stopping.

1 As you approach the ball on the ground, keep your eyes fixed on it and slow down slightly. Make your last stride a long one with your left leg. Plant your left foot next to the left side of the ball.

Take a long approach stride as you prepare to scoop up the ball.

Left-handed players
If you are left-handed, hold this page up to a mirror to see the easiest sequence for you.

2 Leaning forwards, spread the fingers of your right (back) hand and swing it forwards. Place this hand about one-third of the way along the right side of the ball. Pushing your fingers underneath, scoop the ball into your front hand.

Scoop with the back hand into the front hand.

Bring the ball up to your chest and adjust your hands if necessary.

3 Now that you have the ball in both hands, pull it up to your chest as you accelerate away. Adjust your hands on the ball to the normal carrying grip (see page 16).

Two-handed grip
Always carry the ball in both hands. You then have the option to pass left or right or to kick. With two hands on the ball you are more likely to retain possession when you are tackled.

Taking a high ball

High balls are not easy to take but you should always try to catch them cleanly. If you let the ball bounce, it could go anywhere. As the ball comes down, stretch your arms up and watch it all the way into your hands. Let your fingers catch the ball and bring it into your chest. As you land, bend your knees to make a firm base, ready to run, kick, or even to brace yourself for a tackle as the opposition runs towards you.

Bend your knees as you catch the ball to avoid dropping it.

Plant both feet firmly on the ground with a wide stance for maximum stability.

Making a mark

You win a free kick if you catch a high ball cleanly and shout "Mark!" in your own 22 metre (25 yard) area. As the ball drops towards you, spread your legs, reach up, and take the ball in both hands, drawing it into your chest. As you take the ball, bend your knees and loudly shout "Mark!" for the referee to hear.

Watch the ball right into your arms and call "Mark!" Then bring the ball into your chest.

Running with the ball

GOOD RUNNING is essential to success in rugby. You do not have to be a fast sprinter but you do need to be an effective runner to get the ball down over the opposition goal line. Firstly, learn to run straight and secondly, avoid collisions. Look for gaps in the defence and if you cannot find one, wrong-foot your opponents by timing your passes for a team-mate to continue the attack. Equally useful is the ability to change pace by slowing and then accelerating away.

Run in a straight line and be aware of other players. Hold the ball in the normal carrying grip.

Straight running

The quickest way to the goal line is to run straight. When you see a defender in front of you, it is tempting to run across the pitch. However, it is very easy for the other side to defend against this move. If you find yourself drifting sideways, turn quickly to get back to a straight run.

Committing a defender

The key to good attacking moves is pulling defenders out of position. This creates extra space for other support players to run into and continue the attack. This is known as fixing the defender.

The attacker moves left to draw the defender.

The defender moves out of position to cover the attacker.

1 Begin an attack by running straight. Do not assume that you can simply outrun the defender. Instead, you must try to outwit your opponent. Here, the red attacker moves to the left as he approaches the defender.

The attacker has already passed the ball.

The defender tackles too late.

The defender is totally committed as the attacker passes the ball.

2 The attacker has moved left, away from the direction of the support runner to whom he wishes to pass. The defender commits himself to the tackle, but before he can bring the attacker down, the attacker passes to his right.

Always look for
gaps in the defence.

Running into a gap

Here, the blue attacker has run straight but has come up against two defenders. By leaning right, he has convinced both of them that he is going to run past on the right. However, with a sudden swerve to the left, the attacker has wrong-footed the nearest defender. The other defender, thinking that his team-mate would make the tackle, has failed to come across and the attacker can sprint through the gap.

This player will catch
the ball and run
through the gap.

3 The pass is cleanly away and the supporting attacker is clear to receive the ball and accelerate into the gap left by the defender. The first attacker has effectively acted as a decoy to draw the defender away from his team-mate. This tactic is very effective when used by the back five players in any team (see pages 26–27).

Loop running

With loop running, players can take part in an attacking movement more than once. When you have run forwards and passed the ball, look for an opportunity to rejoin the attack further down the line. This is a way of creating an "overlap", or more attackers than defenders.

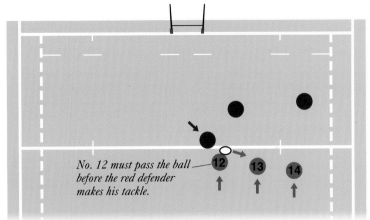

No. 12 must pass the ball
before the red defender
makes his tackle.

1 Three blue attackers are beginning to move forwards, and the red defenders are starting to come across to try to stop the movement. The ball-carrier (No. 12) needs to pass before he is tackled and looks to the nearest support player (No. 13).

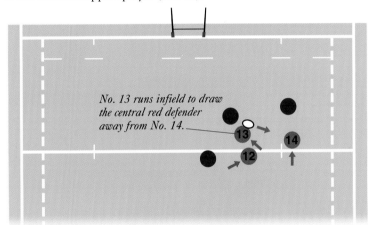

No. 13 runs infield to draw
the central red defender
away from No. 14.

2 The original ball-carrier (No. 12) has passed the ball to his team-mate (No. 13), who now runs infield to draw the central red defender away from the winger (No. 14). The original ball-carrier (No. 12) loops around behind No. 13, ready to rejoin the attack.

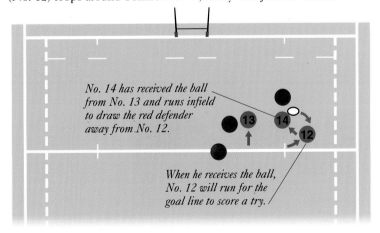

No. 14 has received the ball
from No. 13 and runs infield
to draw the red defender
away from No. 12.

When he receives the ball,
No. 12 will run for the
goal line to score a try.

3 No. 12 has now sprinted around behind the new ball-carrier (No. 14). The blue team is in a strong position with two attackers against the last red defender, who can only tackle one player. No. 14 runs infield to draw him away before passing the ball to No. 12.

Passing

ONCE YOU HAVE LEARNT how to hold and run with the ball, you need to know how to pass it on to a team-mate. In rugby, you must always pass to the side or backwards. A forward pass is not allowed. The success of your team could depend on the speed and accuracy of your passes.

Scissors pass

A scissors pass changes the direction of your attack. Use it when you are running out of space at the side of the pitch or to wrong-foot a defender.

Defender   *You*   *Team-mate*

1 As you run towards an opposition defender, start to move diagonally as if to run between the defender and your team-mate. This will draw the defender towards you, creating a space behind the defender.

You have thrown the ball.

2 As you come across in front of your team-mate, twist at the waist and throw the ball up gently into your team-mate's chest and hands. The ball is hidden from the defender as you pass it.

Your team-mate has the ball.   *The defender has been beaten.*

3 Your team-mate now has the ball and accelerates past the defender, who is wrong-footed and not in a tackling position. There is now space behind the defender for your team-mate to continue the attack.

Always pass with both hands to control the speed and direction of the ball.

Lateral pass

The most basic passing movement is the lateral pass. Practise it until you can perform the pass as effectively from right to left as from left to right – you will need to do both in a rugby match. Most passes are made on the run, at speed, and with a defender in front of you trying to stop your progress. Your coach will help you to prepare for these conditions when you are training.

1 As soon as you notice that a pass is the best way for your team to progress, look for your target receiver. Move the ball from your normal carrying position (see page 16) and bring it down to your side, away from your target.

Take care
Never pass to team-mates who are likely to be tackled as they receive the ball.

Reverse pass

This is a difficult but useful pass if you find yourself standing still with no support players on either side. Instead of passing left or right, throw the ball under your arm to a team-mate behind you. For this you will need strong arms and shoulders and a lot of practice. This pass surprises your opponents and gets you out of trouble.

Finish with your arms pointing at the target. The best pass arrives at chest height, just in front of the receiver.

The attacking player has made the passing movement too obvious.

The defender has intercepted the ball.

Intercepting a pass

Timing your passes is a critical skill. You must draw the defender towards you before you pass or the defender may still stop the team-mate you pass to. A defender who has not been drawn towards you could anticipate your pass and catch it in mid-flight. An interception often leads to a player running up the pitch and scoring a try because of the unexpected switch from defence to attack.

Joost van der Westhuizen, the South African scrum-half, executes a perfect diving pass.

2 Swing your arms and the ball smoothly across your body and aim them at your target. As you extend your arms fully, flick your wrists and fingers to propel the ball towards your team-mate.

Diving pass

The scrum-half is almost the only position to use a diving pass. It is effective when there is intense pressure to get a pass away, often when the ball has not come cleanly from a line-out or a scrum or the scrum-half has to run a few steps to gather the ball. As you reach the ball, place your stronger foot behind it, scoop it up with both hands, and dive forwards using your stronger leg to push off. Swing your arms to throw the ball towards your target receiver.

Tackling

A GOOD TACKLE stops your opponent making progress and this can help your team win matches. For this reason, every young player must learn how to tackle effectively. As the opposition may attack from any angle, you must be able to tackle from the front, the rear, and the side. When your opponents realize that they will be tackled every time they have the ball, they will lose confidence and be more likely to make mistakes.

Front tackle

A front tackle requires courage as your opponent runs straight towards you. It helps if you start to run before you make the tackle, otherwise you could be wrong-footed when the ball-carrier suddenly changes direction.

1 As the ball-carrier approaches, drop into a low position. Check to see if your opponent has changed direction. Lift your shoulders, put your head to one side, and wrap your arms around your opponent's thighs.

Crouch down with your arms around your opponent's upper thighs.

Side tackle

In the side tackle, you position your head behind the ball-carrier's hips and wrap your arms around the top of your opponent's legs. Hit the side of the hips with your shoulder and as the ball-carrier falls forwards, land on top with your head well clear. Get to your feet as quickly as possible after you have made the tackle.

The ball-carrier is falling to the ground.

Firmly grasp the legs to stop the ball-carrier from running forwards.

Rear tackle

When tackling from the rear, you will be running faster than the ball-carrier. Your greater speed ensures that you will come out on top after the tackle. As you make contact, be sure to keep your head away from the ball-carrier's feet. If you tackle with conviction, you will soon master this technique.

1 As you catch the ball-carrier, place your head to one side of your opponent's hips. With your last stride, drive your shoulder into the ball-carrier's buttocks and throw your arms around the upper legs.

Keep your head to one side and make contact with your shoulder.

Land on top of your opponent with your head clear.

Be ready to jump up and take possession of the ball.

2 If the ball-carrier's momentum is greater than yours, simply hold on tightly, and sit back as your opponent falls over your shoulder. With practice, you will time your tackle perfectly and drive your opponent backwards.

3 With the force of your tackle, the ball-carrier will fall back onto his or her side and shoulder and you should land on top with your head clear. If your opponent has dropped the ball, you are in the perfect position to get to your feet quickly, pick up the ball, and start an attacking move for your team.

Your opponent has lost control of the ball.

2 Grip the ball-carrier's legs tightly with your arms so your opponent cannot continue to run. In this situation, all ball-carriers have forward momentum that will make them fall forwards.

When not to tackle
You cannot tackle a player who does not have the ball. In addition, you are not allowed to tackle a player who is jumping to catch the ball, as this could be dangerous.

3 As the ball-carrier falls, continue to grip tightly and keep your head pressed firmly against the side of the buttocks. If you start to slide down the legs, grip more tightly with your arms.

Keep a firm grip as the ball-carrier overbalances.

Your arms are still gripping even though they have slid down the ball-carrier's legs.

A safe landing
If you are being tackled, try to hold on to the ball. Avoid putting out a hand to break your fall, as you could hurt your arm in this way. You must release the ball as soon as you are on the ground.

Team structure – front five

E ACH TEAM has 15 players, made up of eight forwards and seven backs. Forwards, numbered from 1 to 8, tend to be solid and strong, while the backs, numbered from 9 to 15, are generally fast runners. The first five forward players are also known as the front five. The main responsibility of the front five is to obtain possession of the ball at scrums, line-outs, rucks, and mauls.

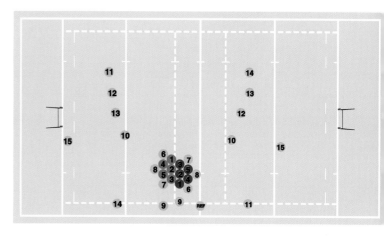

Stage 1 – front five scrum positions

This diagram, which represents the photograph below, shows the referee with two teams ready for a scrum. The front five in each team are highlighted and are central to the scrum. The two locks in the second row support the props and the hooker in the front row. Both hookers try to hook the ball back to gain possession for their team.

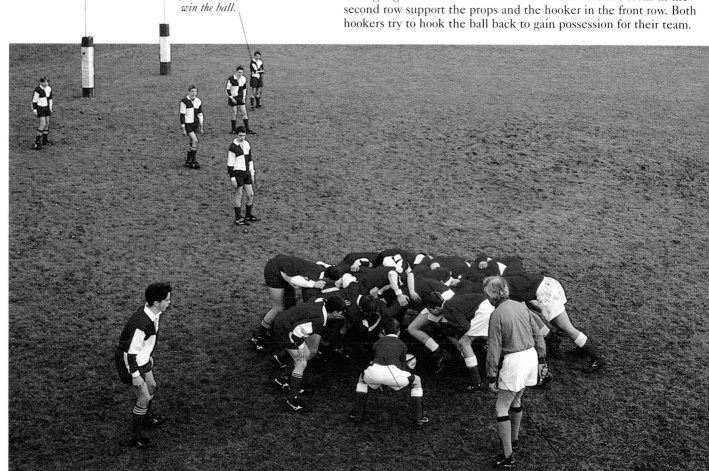

The whole team is in position waiting for the front five to win the ball.

The scrum-half is ready to throw the ball into the scrum.

The front five form the main body of the scrum. They are supported by the other forwards.

Stage 1 – front five win the ball

This photograph is the first in a sequence of three, continued on the following pages. A scrum shows the whole team in action as each player has a specific role. Here, the players are waiting for the scrum to begin as soon as the scrum-half has thrown the ball into the tunnel. The props are supporting the hooker at the front of the scrum, forming a solid platform for the locks to push the scrum forwards.

Props – No. 1 and No. 3

The props support the hooker in the scrum. No. 1, on the hooker's left, is the "loose-head". No. 3, on the right, is the "tight-head" because this player's head goes between two opposition players' heads. In line-outs the props protect the taller jumpers in their team. They are often the strongest players but must also be quick to reach rucks and mauls and drive the opposition back.

The backs are lined up ready to receive the ball.

Victor Ubogu, the England tight-head prop, gets ready for a scrum against Australia.

Jason Leonard, the loose-head prop, stands on the left of Brian Moore, the hooker.

Hooker – No. 2

A key player in every team, the hooker has two main duties. The first is to strike the ball quickly during scrums and heel it back to the waiting scrum-half. Secondly, the hooker throws the ball in at line-outs. The ability to throw accurately is essential for the team to retain possession of the ball. Hookers have strong arms and shoulders and are quick to lead the forwards in attack or defence.

The locks are the highest jumpers in a line-out.

Locks – No. 4 and No. 5

The tallest players in the team, the two locks form the second row in a scrum and are the main pushing force. In a line-out they are the highest jumpers and one of them will usually catch the ball and pass it to the scrum-half. Because of their height, locks are often first to catch the ball at kick-off and they must be brave to stand up to opposition forwards when they land with the ball in their hands.

Team structure – middle five

THE MIDDLE FIVE players are the heart of the team. They include three forwards and two backs. The front five must win possession of the ball but it is the middle five who are responsible for using it effectively. They can do this by starting a running attack or kicking to drive the other team back towards their own goal line. The middle five are also the first line of defence if the other team wins the ball at a scrum or a line-out.

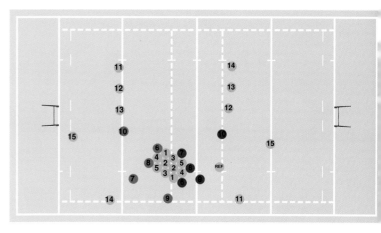

Stage 2 – middle five scrum positions

In this diagram, which represents the photograph below, the middle five in each team are highlighted just as the scrum ends. The two flankers bind on to the sides of the scrum and the No. 8 positioned at the back of the scrum. These three are often known as the back row. The two backs in the middle five are the scrum-half and the fly-half.

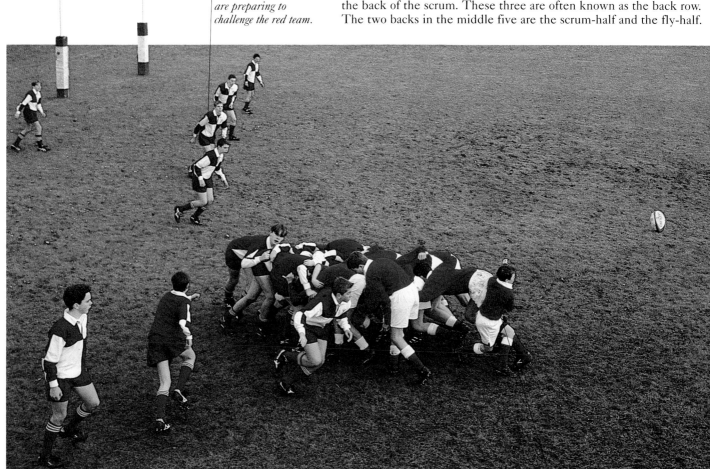

The blue team's backs are preparing to challenge the red team.

The red scrum-half is passing the ball to the fly-half.

Stage 2 – middle five use the ball

Here, the middle five players are in action. After the scrum was formed, the red scrum-half put the ball into the tunnel. The red flankers supported the scrum and did not need to defend as the ball came back cleanly through their own scrum. The No. 8 kept the ball at his feet until the scrum-half was in position and ready to pick it up. Now the red scrum-half passes the ball to the fly-half, who can decide how to attack.

The New Zealand flanker, Mark Carter, tries to tackle the ball-carrier.

Stephen Larkham of Australia resists the tackle.

Gary Teichmann, the South African No. 8, breaks from a scrum.

Flankers – No. 6 and No. 7

When the opposition wins the ball in a scrum or line-out, the flankers are normally the first players to defend, so they must relish tackling. They protect the sides of the scrum in this way, and also the back of the line-out. In addition, they must be vigorous and quick attackers, supporting rolling mauls or joining in their attacking back line when necessary in order to outnumber the opposition defenders.

No. 8

The No. 8 is the anchor in the scrum. As the ball comes back, the No. 8 keeps it at his or her feet until the scrum-half is ready to take it. Occasionally, the No. 8 starts an attack by picking the ball up at the back of the scrum and running at the defence. As the No. 8 passes the scrum, the flanker will break off in support.

The red fly-half is about to receive the ball.

Scrum-half – No. 9

The link between the forwards and the backs, the scrum-half's first role is to put the ball into the scrum and then run around to pick it up and pass it on to the fly-half. At line-outs, the scrum-half is the only non-forward player allowed to stand nearby, ready to receive the ball from one of the jumpers. Every scrum-half must be able to catch, pass, and kick quickly and accurately.

The fly-half is often the team's main place kicker.

Fly-half – No. 10

The fly-half is the play-maker in every team and must decide how to attack as soon the ball is received. Every fly-half will look for a gap to run through, a chance to pass to a centre player, or may kick the ball over the heads of the opposition for a winger to reach. The other key role for a fly-half is often as the team's place kicker, taking conversions and penalty kicks at goal.

Team structure – back five

THE BACK FIVE players are the main attacking unit as well as the last line of defence in any rugby team. The middle five begin most attacks but the backs must make the most of their chances to score. With good running and handling skills, the back five normally score more tries than other players. However, when the other team has the ball the backs must provide solid defence and bring their tackling skills into play.

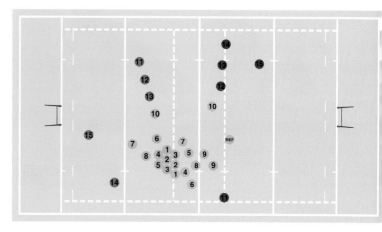

Stage 3 – back five scrum positions

The back five in each team are highlighted in this diagram, which represents the photograph below. The two wingers attack or defend along the sides of the pitch. In the middle are two fast-running centres. At the rear of each team is the full-back.

The blue team's backs are preparing to tackle the attacking red backs.

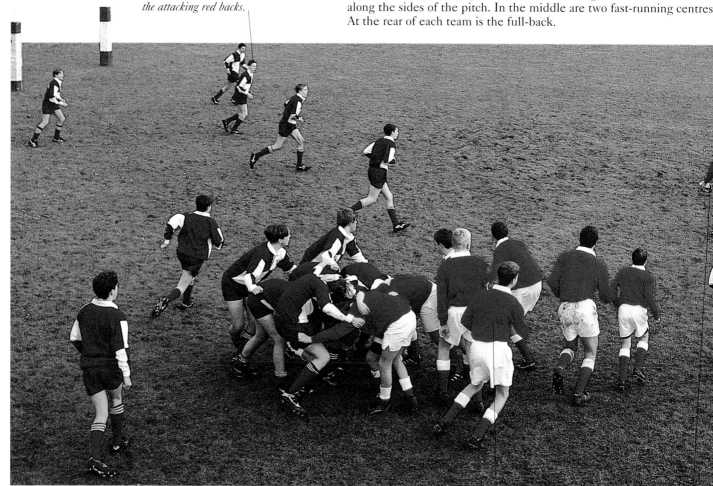

The forwards have broken away from the scrum.

The red fly-half is about to pass the ball to the centre.

Stage 3 – back five attack

Here, the ball has come out of the scrum to the red fly-half, who is passing it to the nearest centre. The centre and right wing are lined up in support. Coming up fast is the full-back, who is hoping to join in the attack, perhaps looping around the right wing to create an overlap, or act as a dummy to draw defenders away from the centres. The blue team's back five are running forwards to tackle the attacking red backs.

Jonah Lomu of the New Zealand All Blacks runs with the ball.

Wingers – No. 11 and No. 14

Wingers are the fastest players on the field and must have excellent handling, catching, and passing skills. Speed is vital to follow kicks up-field and because they rarely receive a pass with space to attack freely. Normally, wingers try to outrun defenders through narrow gaps close to the touchline. The ability to change direction and pace to avoid tackles are also important skills for wingers.

Centres work together to exploit gaps in the defence.

Centres – No. 12 and No. 13

Centres must be fast runners and good tacklers. They should be clever players, able to work together to create gaps or exploit weaknesses in the opposition defence line. A key role is to pass the ball to the wingers quickly but also to make space for them to run into. Centres can do this by running infield slightly before they pass to draw defenders away from the touchline.

The full-back tackles to prevent a try being scored.

Full-back – No. 15

All full-backs must be brave as they often make the last tackle to stop a try being scored. When a team is driven backwards by the opposition, the full-back may kick the ball long and high down the field. As the last position, the full-back often catches high balls with the opposition running in to challenge. As well as these defensive duties, the full-back must constantly look for opportunities to join in an attack.

The referee is keeping up with the action and following the progress of the ball.

Kick-off and drop-out

THE KICK-OFF is a place kick from the centre of the halfway line. It is taken at the beginning of the game and again at the start of the second half. After one team has scored, the other team kicks off from the halfway line with a drop kick. A drop-out restarts the game after the ball has gone dead over the goal line. The defending team takes a drop kick from behind their 22 m (25 yd) line to continue play.

The red team's fly-half has taken the kick-off.

Ball

Kick-off

Before your team kicks off, make sure that you are all behind the halfway line with your backs lined up to defend and your forwards ready to follow up as the ball is kicked. The ball must go at least 10 m (10 yd) from the kick-off.

Attack from kick-off

A kick-off is an opportunity to attack. A long kick sends the opposition back into their own half and a short kick gives your forwards a chance to catch the ball as it lands, putting pressure on the opposition.

This player must get behind the ball or he will be offside.

The blue player prepares to take the catch.

1 The red team has taken the kick-off with a long kick, which almost reaches the opposition 22 m (25 yd) line. The red forwards cannot run fast enough to be under the ball, so the blue players, who are well positioned, should win it.

The red forward has to defend against the blue attack.

Blue forwards come together to support the ball-carrier.

2 One of the blue forwards has caught the ball cleanly and is already moving up the pitch supported by blue team-mates. The red team has lost a potential attacking opportunity and they must now prepare to defend.

The red forwards are following up as the ball is kicked.

The red players stand ready to attack behind the player who kicks the ball.

22 metre drop-out

If a ball that was last touched by an attacking player goes into the in-goal area and is touched down by a defender, the defending team restarts the game with a drop-out from behind their 22 m (25 yd) line. A drop kick must cross your 22 m (25 yd) line, where the opposition can stand. If the ball goes over the dead-ball line, the defending team can choose to restart with a drop-out or a scrum from where the ball was last kicked. As you kick the ball, your team-mates must be behind you. A short kick that they can reach quickly is a good tactic.

Jumping for the ball

Here, the US team has kicked off in a World Cup match from 1991 and the English forwards are receiving the ball. One of the US forwards has reached the ball as it lands and is jumping among the English forwards. He is hoping to catch the ball himself or disrupt the English catch, preventing an attacking movement.

The US lock, Kevin Swords, tries to disrupt the catch.

This English forward tries to catch the ball cleanly.

This player cannot tackle unless the US forward lands with the ball.

Scrums

A SCRUM IS A TRIAL of strength. It is also the most recognizable feature of a game of rugby. The referee calls for a scrum after a minor infringement of the rules, such as a forward pass or an accidental knock-on when a player drops the ball. All eight forwards and the scrum-half from each team try to win the ball without handling it. Only by pushing or hooking the ball back with the feet can a team gain possession so that the scrum-half can start an attack.

The head of the loose-head prop is on the outside of the scrum.

Front row binding

Each front row is made up of the hooker, whose arms come around and bind on to the props on either side. Tight-head props (above left) must bind on the opposition loose-head prop (above right) with the outside arm and clench that prop's shirt without pulling down. Loose-head props must do the same or rest the hand on their leg.

Scrum positions

The eight players on each side of the scrum are the forwards. To form the scrum, the hookers hold up their arms and their props bind on to them. The locks bind together and push their heads either side of the hookers' hips. The No. 8s then join in at the back and the flankers bind on either side of the locks. When both sets of forwards are ready and the ball is in the scrum-half's hands, the referee will ask the two teams to come together by calling "engage".

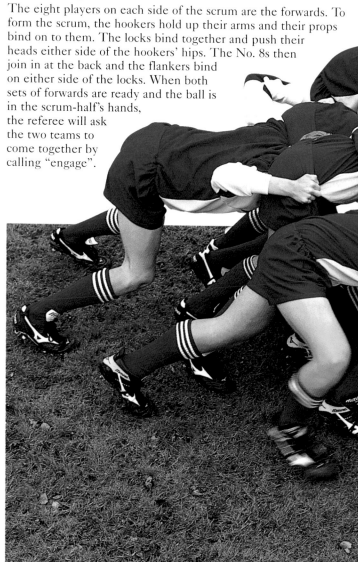

Hooking the ball back

The front row is the solid platform for the whole scrum so props and hookers are usually strong and stocky. Tight binding is essential and hookers must grip their props' shirts firmly under the armpits and pull them in to them. Here the hooker stands on the left foot, turns towards the loose-head prop, and hooks the ball back through the prop's legs with the right foot.

All the players' shoulders must be higher than their hips.

Using a scrum machine

Winning your own scrum ensures that your team gains possession of the ball for an attack. This requires close teamwork by all eight forwards and your coach will teach you the correct techniques for safe scrummaging. This is vital as the scrum is the most physical set piece with close contact between many players.

Winning the ball

When the scrum has formed, the scrum-half of the team that has been awarded the put-in stands 1 m (1 yd) away from the scrum. Then the scrum-half throws the ball into the tunnel between the two front rows in a single movement.

The scrum ends as soon as the ball is picked up at the back.

The scrum-half who is not putting the ball in must not interfere.

1 The scrum-half throws the ball into the tunnel. It is normal to throw in from the side next to that team's loose-head prop because their hooker is nearer than the opposition hooker and is more likely to win the ball. Once the ball enters the tunnel, both hookers strike for it with their feet and try to direct the ball back through their own side of the scrum. The other players attempt to push their opponents back, away from the ball.

2 If your hooker's strike has been successful, or if you have pushed the other team away, the ball will be available at the back of your team's scrum. From here your scrum-half can pick up the ball and start an attack by passing, kicking, or running with it. All the players must stay bound on to the scrum until the scrum-half picks up the ball. Sometimes, as a variation, the No. 8 picks up the ball.

Scrum safety
Never pull downwards during a scrum or allow it to collapse as this could be dangerous for you or other players.

No. 1, the loose-head prop, stands on the hooker's left.

No. 2, the hooker, is the only player who can strike for the ball.

No. 3, the tight-head prop, must be solid to prevent the scrum wheeling around.

No. 4, a lock, is a powerful pusher in the second row.

No. 5, a lock, should be of a similar height and build to the No. 4.

No. 6, a flanker, is a pusher but is also ready to attack or defend.

No. 7, a flanker, performs a similar role to the No. 6.

The No. 8 is a solid anchor at the back and is ready to control the ball for the scrum-half.

Line-outs

W HEN THE BALL crosses the touchline, the referee restarts the game with a line-out. Normally, the team that did not put the ball into touch takes the throw-in. The hooker throws in from where the ball crossed the touchline and up to seven forwards line up on the pitch. The same number of opposition forwards stand beside them. Then the hooker throws the ball straight down the middle of the lines and the players jump to try and catch it.

The gap between the two lines is 1 m (1 yd) wide.

The scrum-half stands ready to receive the ball.

The backs must stay at least 10 m (10 yd) from the line-out.

The forwards line up from 5 m (5 yd) to 15 m (16 yd) from the touchline.

The opposition hooker is not in the line-out and can stand closer than 5 m (5 yd) from the thrower.

Throw-in

The accuracy of the throw-in determines the success of the line-out. Hookers should vary the speed, height, and distance of their throws. They will need to drop the ball straight into the outstretched hands of their jumpers, no matter where they are.

Waiting for the throw-in

A prop stands at the front of the line-out, often facing away from the hooker, ready to support an attack by the forwards if necessary. The two tallest players in each team stand in second place and fourth or fifth position. All hookers call code words to tell their team where the ball will go.

Grip the ball near the rear point.

Bend your arms to pull back as far as you can.

1 Hold the ball high and point it straight down the middle of the line-out. Lean backwards to increase your throwing speed and keep looking at the point that your jumper will reach on leaping into the air.

Keep your front foot behind the touchline.

2 Bring the ball back behind your head with both hands and move your body forwards, holding on to the ball as long as possible.

Extend your arms straight out and aim at your target as you release the ball.

3 Aim both hands and release the ball at the last moment when you are at full stretch. This helps to achieve greatest accuracy, straight down the middle of the line-out.

Your momentum should carry you over the line onto the pitch, ready to join in.

Winning the ball

If you catch the ball, you can pass it back to the waiting scrum-half, or bring the ball into your chest and turn away from the opposition. The other forwards can then close around you and form a maul to drive forwards. This is a good tactic when you are very close to the opposite goal line.

Use the palm of your hand to tap the ball back.

The referee is well positioned to ensure fair play.

The blue player who is jumping knows that the hooker has aimed the ball at him.

The red player has jumped well but has missed this ball.

Palming the ball

Winning "clean ball" by catching it in both hands is always best as it is under your control. However, if it is not your team's throw-in, it is often very effective to jump and stretch with your inside arm, tapping the ball back to your scrum-half with the palm of your hand.

The hooker who threw the ball in has stepped onto the pitch.

Quick throw-in
As an alternative to the line-out, under certain circumstances, a player can choose to take a quick throw-in to restart the game. This often catches the opposition by surprise.

Tries, conversions, and goals

TO WIN A GAME of rugby, your team must score more points than the opposition. The referee awards points for scoring a try or kicking a goal. You score tries by touching the ball down over your opponents' goal line and any player can experience the excitement of diving past the other team's defenders. You score goals by kicking the ball directly over your opponents' crossbar and between the goal posts. There are three types of goal that you can score: a conversion, a drop goal, and a penalty goal.

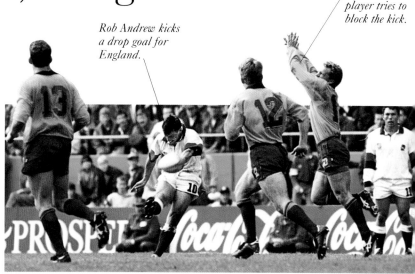

Rob Andrew kicks a drop goal for England.

This Australia player tries to block the kick.

Drop goal

Any player can score a drop goal at any time during a game. When you find yourself close enough to your opponents' goal line, you can try a drop kick at their goal (see pages 36–37). If the ball goes over the bar and through the posts, you score three points. Here, Rob Andrew drop kicks to win the quarter final of the 1995 Rugby World Cup against Australia.

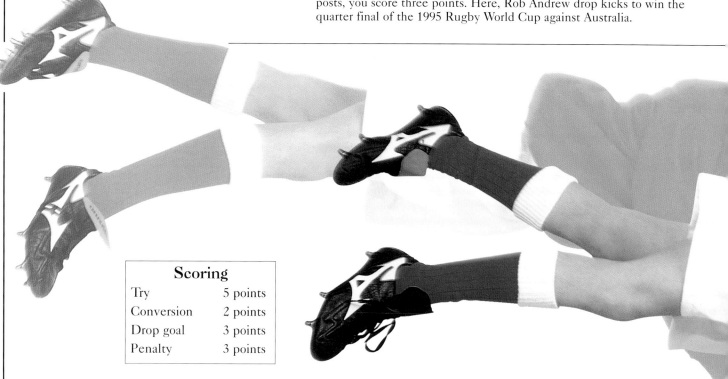

Scoring	
Try	5 points
Conversion	2 points
Drop goal	3 points
Penalty	3 points

Scoring a try

There is nothing more satisfying than diving over your opponents' goal line and touching the ball down to score a try. You do not even have to take the ball there yourself. If the ball has gone over your opponents' goal line and you are the first player to touch it down before it goes over the touchline or the dead-ball line, your team scores five points. You can also score if your scrum, ruck, or maul moves over the opponents' goal line and you drop onto the ball on the ground. You must always push the ball down with your hand, arm, or body from your neck to your waist.

Controlling the ball
Be sure to hold the ball firmly and press downwards as it touches the ground for a try. You will not score if you drop or bounce the ball as you are touching it down.

Penalty goal

If one of your opponents commits an offence against the laws of the game, such as an obstruction or an offside, the referee will award your team a penalty where the offence occurred. When this is close to your opponents' goal, you can take a penalty kick at goal. This can be a place kick or a drop kick and if it is successful it scores three points.

This conversion has gone straight between the posts.

Normally, the fly-half or the full-back takes all place kicks.

Most players choose a place kick for a penalty kick at goal.

Converting a try

After your team has scored a try, you are given a free kick at goal. If the ball goes over the bar and between the posts, this is called a conversion and scores two extra points. The kick can be a place kick or a drop kick (see pages 36–37). It is taken from anywhere in front of the posts but no further in from the touchline than where the ball was touched down for the try. Here, Neil Jenkins, the Welsh fly-half, has converted a try against Scotland in a Five Nations championship match.

Your hand, arm, or body must push down on the ball.

The ball must touch the ground over the goal line.

Goal line

Kicking

RUGBY PLAYERS USE a variety of kicks, each for a specific purpose. The fly-half or the full-back will take most place kicks and drop kicks and the scrum-half will normally take other kicks. However, all players should be able to perform a grubber kick or punt the ball up the pitch, so you should learn the techniques shown here for defensive and attacking play.

Left-footed kickers
The kicks shown here are for right-footed players. To see a left-footed kick, hold this page up to a mirror.

Place kick

A place kick is taken with the ball on the ground and is used to start the game from the centre of the halfway line. It is also used for a conversion attempt after a try has been scored and for a penalty kick at goal. Most teams have a specialist kicker for all place kicks, usually the fly-half or the full-back.

1 Place the ball vertically on the tee or angle it slightly towards the target. Look at the ball and the target several times to ensure that they are lined up. Stand with your left foot beside the ball. Take three large steps backwards, starting with your right foot.

Keep your eyes fixed firmly on the ball.

Strike the ball with your instep.

Your weight is on your left leg.

2 Run forwards, planting your left foot alongside the ball. Keep your eyes fixed on the ball and strike it firmly with the instep of your right foot. Follow through with your right leg, ending up high and pointing at the target.

Drop kick

If a player is aware of the opportunity, a drop kick can be one of the easiest ways of scoring in rugby. It is also used to restart the match from the 22 m line (25 yd line) after the ball has gone dead over the goal line.

1 Hold the ball upright in both hands and drop it straight to the ground. Do not be tempted to throw the ball up before you drop it as this could make your kick less accurate.

Use your arms to help you balance.

Focus on the point where the ball will hit the ground.

Hold the ball vertically before you drop it straight down.

Strike the ball with the laced area of your boot.

2 Transfer your weight to your left leg. Lean back slightly so that your right leg is free to swing smoothly and cleanly. Strike the ball with your right foot immediately after it hits the ground.

Grubber kick

During a match, any player can perform a grubber kick. It is an effective attacking kick that drives the ball along the ground, bouncing end over end. The ball can be difficult for defenders to control as it comes bouncing towards them and often leads to a knock-on (see page 14) when a player tries to catch it. This kick turns defence into attack, so you are often under pressure as you take it.

1 Hold the ball in front of your knee, and prepare to drop it straight down. You will kick the ball just before it hits the ground.

Hold the ball low and drop it vertically.

2 Point your toes at the ground and strike the upper half of the ball with the laced area of your boot. This propels the ball firmly along the ground. At the point of contact, your knee should be over the ball.

Strike with the laced area of your boot.

3 As soon as you strike the ball, look at the target and follow through with your kicking leg. As your foot follows through, it points at the target and ends up at head height.

A high follow-through improves the accuracy of your kick.

Punt

A punt is a kick to give distance or height. Start by holding the ball level with your waist with one hand on top and one underneath. Allow the ball to drop without rolling or twisting. As it falls, strike the middle of the ball with the area of your boot just above the laces. The higher the ball is when you kick it, the higher it is likely to travel. This gives your team-mates more time to reach it and puts pressure on the opposition.

Use both feet
Practise kicking with both feet. In a match, you will need to react quickly with the foot nearest the ball.

Keep your eyes on the ball as you strike it.

Aim for good height as you make contact with the ball.

Strike the middle of the ball using the point above your laces.

Rucks and mauls

ALTHOUGH THEY CAN look like informal scrums, rucks and mauls involve specific team skills and require careful coaching. They are used to retain possession of the ball and often begin when a ball-carrier is tackled. If the player remains standing, a maul can be formed. However, if the player and ball end up on the ground, a ruck develops. In a ruck the ball cannot be handled but in a maul it is always held.

The red player has stopped you.

Hold the ball away from the tackler and in clear view of your team-mates.

All players must keep their heads up, ready for the contact.

Ruck

As soon as a ball is on the ground and players from each team are in physical contact over it, a ruck has been formed. Players join at the back and bind together for strength, driving in and forcing their opponents away from the ball. Players must not handle the ball until it finally emerges from the ruck.

1 Prepare for contact with a long stride to lower your shoulder and give yourself a firm stance. Turn your shoulder in and try to bump your opponent away. Try to stay on your feet if possible.

Protect your head, face, and ears.

Maul

Often a maul develops after a forward has caught the ball in a line-out. The catcher turns away from the opposition and starts a maul, knowing that team-mates are nearby. The ball-carrier must remain standing. Mauls are effective near the opposition goal line as the ball-carrier, once over the line, can drop to the ground and score a try.

1 You are the blue player carrying the ball. The red player is holding you and the first blue support player has arrived. The blue support player puts his hands on the ball to make it more secure.

2 More support players arrive. Another blue player has taken the ball from you and blue players protect the new ball-carrier from the opposition. Red players bind together to stop the blue players from driving forwards.

The red support tries to stop the maul from moving forwards.

The first support player makes sure that there are four hands protecting the ball.

You are in the centre of the maul, holding the ball.

The red player tries to free the ball.

2 You could not stay on your feet and have gone to ground, placing the ball as near to your own team-mates as possible. The ruck is now formed and the ball must not be handled. Support players should bind together to form the ruck and hold their heads up.

Players bind together as if in a scrum.

3 The support players from both sides bind together to form a strong unit. Here, the attacking blue players are driving their opponents away from you and the ball.

Support players must keep their shoulders above their hips.

You must move away as soon as it is safe to do so.

The red players have been pushed away from the ball.

4 The blue players have successfully rucked their opponents off the ball. The blue scrum-half can pick up the ball as soon as it emerges from the back of the ruck, ready to launch a new attack and set up a try.

The scrum-half picks up the ball as soon as it is clear of the ruck.

Push the ball in one move towards the support and then remove your hand.

The new ball-carrier protects the ball.

You are now turned and driving the maul forwards.

Support must arrive quickly to get the maul rolling forwards.

3 The blue team is moving the maul forwards and the new ball-carrier can either retain possession or make the ball available for the scrum-half.

Use it or lose it!
If your team has the ball in a maul, you must make progress or the referee will award a scrum to the other side.

The new ball-carrier holds the ball as far as possible from the red players.

The red team has been pushed backwards.

The ball is now available for the blue scrum-half, who will pass, kick, or run.

Retaining possession

YOUR TEAM must hold on to the ball to score tries and win matches. Good rugby is all about continuity. That means that your side must retain possession for as long as possible. Once the ball is in your control, be sure to make progress towards the opposition goal line. When you combine techniques to avoid tackles with good passing and handling skills, you will score impressive tries.

Dummy pass

As you run with the ball, you will often come up against a defender. Before passing the ball, run towards the defender to draw your opponent to you and away from your team-mate. However, sometimes the defender expects you to pass and will not commit to tackling you. This is the time to "sell a dummy", or pretend to make a pass.

Team-mate

Pull your arms back as with a normal pass.

Defender

1 As you approach the defender, hold the ball in front of you in both hands. Move slightly towards your opponent and away from your team-mate. Then pull your arms back exactly as if you were preparing to make a normal pass to your team-mate.

Side-step

The objective of the side-step is to wrong-foot your opponent. You lean and move in one direction before suddenly changing direction and passing the defender on the opposite side to the one he or she expects.

Tuck the ball firmly under your arm.

1 Run straight at your opponent until you are close enough for the defender to start preparing to tackle. Move to your right so that the defender leans left. On your next right-foot stride, plant your foot firmly on the ground and drive off strongly in the other direction.

Bring your right leg across as you drive hard off your left leg.

2 Take a long left-foot stride to move away from your opponent. The defender's weight is on the left foot and he cannot lean right quickly enough to catch you. You are at an advantage when you time the side-step correctly because you only have to change direction. Your opponent, on the other hand, has to stop forward momentum and change direction.

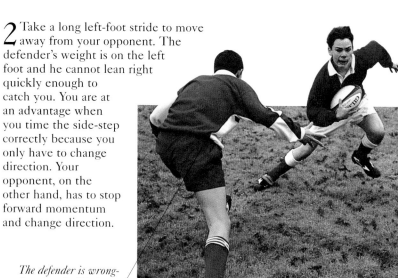

The defender is wrong-footed and off balance.

Swerve

Run straight at the defender, with your weight well balanced and the ball in both hands. Suddenly change direction, in this case by leaning sharply left and bringing your right leg across while driving hard off your left leg. The defender is unlikely to catch you. The swerve is even more effective if you can accelerate sharply at the same time.

Look convincing as you pretend to pass the ball.

The defender is left with no-one to tackle.

Hold the ball firmly and accelerate towards the goal line.

2 Throw your arms across your body to make the pass. If you can see that the defender has not been drawn towards you and is still in a position to tackle your team-mate, do not release the ball. It is important to get ready to pass as you would normally. That way you will persuade your opponent that you are actually going to pass the ball.

3 At the last moment, grip the ball firmly with your fingertips and pull it back into your body. Hold the ball firmly and accelerate away from the defender, who cannot reach to tackle you. If you perform the dummy well, your team-mate should be as surprised as your opponent that you have not passed the ball.

Performing a hand-off

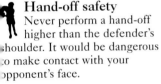

Hand-off safety
Never perform a hand-off higher than the defender's shoulder. It would be dangerous to make contact with your opponent's face.

If you are too late to change direction or your opponent is too close when you receive the ball, the last resort is the hand-off. As the defender crouches to tackle, tuck the ball under your furthest arm and raise your nearest hand. Push your hand onto your opponent's shoulder or upper arm. Then run on, using the shoulder to push yourself away and avoid the tackle.

Carry the ball in the hand that is furthest from your opponent.

Aim your free hand at the defender's shoulder.

Making the ball available

To ensure that your team keeps the ball after you are tackled, hold it firmly in both hands and close to your chest as you fall. Do not put an arm out to break your fall. When you land, turn to face your team-mates and push the ball towards them. A support player can then pick up the ball and continue your team's attack.

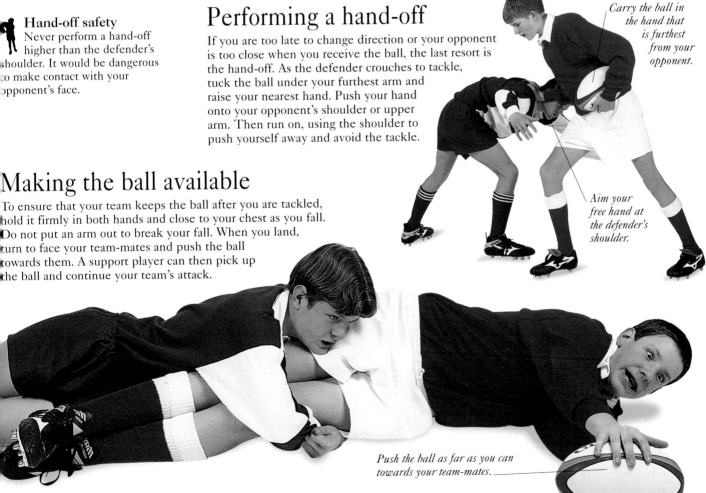

Push the ball as far as you can towards your team-mates.

Taking it further

A S YOUR SKILLS improve, you can take part in rugby competitions against other local teams. Most clubs cater for all ages and abilities and if you continue to play well, you can aspire to join a professional club or even represent your country. Touring overseas is part of rugby tradition and top competitions, such as the Five Nations and the Tri-Nations championships, now attract thousands of enthusiastic spectators.

The referee makes sure that the two teams are ready to form the scrum.

The French forwards bind tightly and prepare to engage the scrum.

Under-19s and under-21s rugby

If you are a talented player, there are opportunities to play for your country from the age of 18. Major rugby-playing nations have now organized under-21s teams. This photograph shows a scrum from the England versus France under-21s match played in May 1998. Under-19s rugby has been established for longer at international level and the thirty-first Junior World Cup for under-19s teams was played in Wales in March 1999.

Waisale Serevi of Fiji breaks away to score against Argentina.

Hong Kong Sevens

Sevens is a variation on the full game of rugby. Sides are limited to seven players each and games last only seven or ten minutes each half. It is a fast game based on running and passing skills and scores are often very high. The Hong Kong International Sevens Tournament, which started in 1976, is the oldest in the world and attracts many spectators from abroad every year.

England lock, Martin Johnson, stretches high to reach the ball.

Five Nations Championship

The annual Five Nations Championship is played between England, Wales, Scotland, Ireland, and France. It is the world's oldest international tournament and the most important competition in the northern hemisphere. It started in 1882 with four nations and has been a yearly competition since France joined in 1910. It will become a Six Nations Championship in 2000 when Italy joins the competition. Here, the English and French forwards are jumping for the ball in a line-out during a match played in France in 1996.

Tri-Nations Championship

The Tri-Nations Championship is contested by Australia, New Zealand, and South Africa. Each country plays the other two both at home and away, and each win is worth two points. To encourage high-scoring games, extra points are awarded to a team that loses narrowly and also to a team that scores more than four tries in a match. The tournament is held in July or August each year. This photograph is from a match between Australia and New Zealand in 1998.

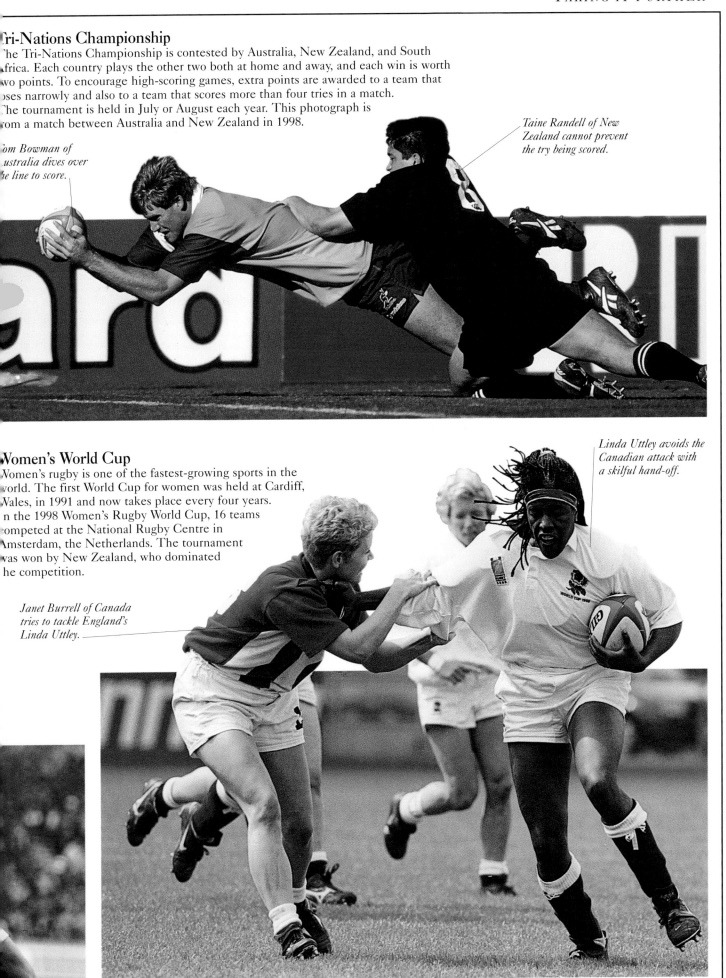

Taine Randell of New Zealand cannot prevent the try being scored.

Tom Bowman of Australia dives over the line to score.

Women's World Cup

Women's rugby is one of the fastest-growing sports in the world. The first World Cup for women was held at Cardiff, Wales, in 1991 and now takes place every four years. In the 1998 Women's Rugby World Cup, 16 teams competed at the National Rugby Centre in Amsterdam, the Netherlands. The tournament was won by New Zealand, who dominated the competition.

Linda Uttley avoids the Canadian attack with a skilful hand-off.

Janet Burrell of Canada tries to tackle England's Linda Uttley.

The World Cup

SINCE THE FIRST World Cup in 1987, rugby has attracted major interest in many countries. The competition began in the southern hemisphere and has also been hosted by Great Britain and South Africa. It is held once every four years and more than 60 countries competed for a place in the 1999 Rugby World Cup. The finals represent the highest level of international rugby and always produce a thrilling spectacle.

The first World Cup

The idea for a Rugby World Cup started in the southern hemisphere and 16 countries were invited to take part in 1987. Most matches were played in New Zealand, with others held in Australia. New Zealand beat France 29–9 in the final at Eden Park in Auckland to become the first ever world champions. In this photograph, the New Zealand captain, David Kirk, dives past Patrice Lagisquet of France to score an impressive try.

Webb Ellis Cup

The Webb Ellis Cup was named after the boy who is credited with inventing the game of rugby in 1823. The 38-cm (15-in) high cup is made of gilded silver and the design is based on an 18th-century trophy. It was won by New Zealand in 1987, Australia in 1991, and South Africa in 1995.

New rugby nations

The World Cup gives teams from countries that are relatively new to rugby the chance to play against the sport's top nations. Here, the Japanese scrum-half, Masami Horikisho, is tackled by Maurice Field of Ireland during a World Cup match at Bloemfontaine, South Africa, in 1995.

Worldwide interest

Rugby increased its profile as a worldwide sport in 1995, the year of the third World Cup. Matches were televised and many viewers became keen fans of rugby for the first time. In this photograph, Yann Delaigue of France tackles a Tongan attacker in a match played at Loftus Versfeld, Pretoria, South Africa. France won the match by 38 points to Tonga's 10 points.

Yann Delaigue of France tries to win possession of the ball.

Nelson Mandela, the South African President, wore the team's colours to watch the World Cup final.

The 1995 World Cup

The South African people were overjoyed when the host nation won the World Cup in 1995. This event marked the return of the country to full international sport following the years of isolation that resulted from South Africa's policy of apartheid. In a dramatic final at Ellis Park in Johannesburg, South Africa played New Zealand, who were the favourites for the Cup. South Africa managed to hold on to their lead and the final score was 15–12 after extra time.

The Springbok's captain, Francois Pienaar, received the Webb Ellis Cup.

Glossary

During practice, or when watching rugby, you may find it helpful to understand some of the following words and phrases.

A

Advantage When the referee allows play to continue after a breach of the laws to see if the non-offending team can benefit.
Attacking team The team that is in possession of the ball.

B

Back five The two wingers, two centres, and the full-back, who wear numbers 11 to 15.
Back row The two flankers and the No. 8, who wear numbers 6 to 8.
Backs The players who wear numbers 9 to 15.
Ball-carrier The player currently in possession of the ball.
Bind To hold tightly on to other players in your team with your arms during scrums, rucks, and mauls.

C

Centre Each team has two centres, who control the field between the fly-half and the wingers and wear numbers 12 and 13.
Conversion A successful kick at goal after a try has been scored. The ball goes over the opposition crossbar and between the goal posts. This is worth 2 points.
Crossbar The 3-m (10-ft) high bar that connects the goal posts.

D

Dead ball A ball that has gone out of play or over the dead-ball line, or after the referee has blown the whistle.
Defending team The team that does not have the ball.
Drive When forwards bind together and push back their opponents.
Drop goal A drop kick that goes over the opposition crossbar and between the goal posts to score 3 points.
Drop kick A kick where the foot strikes the ball just as it hits the ground after the kicker drops it.

Making a mark

A lateral pass

Drop-out A drop kick by the defending team to restart the game from the 22 m (25 yd) line.
Dummy pass A deliberate deception by the ball-carrier, who pretends to pass but then holds on to the ball.

E

Engage The command from the referee that instructs the two front rows to come together to start the scrum.

F

Flanker Each team has two flankers, who wear numbers 6 and 7, and bind on to the sides of the scrum.
Fly-half The number 10 position who is normally the key decision-maker in the team as well as the place kicker.
Forward pass An illegal pass that goes in the direction of the opponents' goal line.
Forwards The players who wear numbers 1 to 8.
Front five The two props, hooker, and two locks, who wear numbers 1 to 5.
Front row The two props and hooker who engage directly with their opposite numbers at the front of a scrum.
Full-back The number 15 position, who is normally the last line of defence.

G

Goal line The line that you must cross in order to score a try.
Goal posts The upright posts between which the ball must pass to score a goal.
Grubber kick A kick that rolls along the ground.

H

Hand-off Pushing an opponent away by the shoulder to avoid a tackle.

Hooker The player who wears the number 2 shirt, stands in the front row of the scrum, and hooks the ball back.

I

Infringement Any action that is against the laws of the game.
In-goal area The area between the goal line and the dead-ball line where tries may be scored.

K

Kick-off A place kick from the centre of the halfway line to start the game or a drop kick from the same place to restart the game after a score.
Knock-on When the ball travels forwards towards your opponents' goal line after a mishandle or failure to catch cleanly.

L

Lateral pass A normal pass that goes sideways or backwards.
Laws The rules of the game.
Line-out A set piece to restart the game after the ball has gone over the touchline, where the forwards line up for the ball to be thrown in between the two lines.
Lock Each team has two locks, numbers 4 and 5. They are the second row of the scrum and the main jumpers in a line-out.
Loop running Passing the ball and then running around behind the new ball-carrier, ready to receive a return pass.
Loose ball A ball that is on the ground so that a player can pick it up.

M

Mark The call you make when catching a ball cleanly behind your own 22 m (25 yd) line to get a free kick.
Maul When players from each team close around the ball-carrier, who remains standing.

Picking up a loose ball

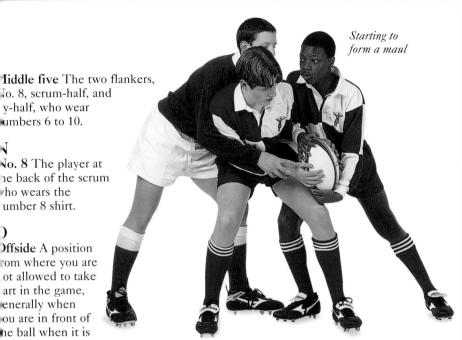

Starting to form a maul

Middle five The two flankers, No. 8, scrum-half, and fly-half, who wear numbers 6 to 10.

N

No. 8 The player at the back of the scrum who wears the number 8 shirt.

O

Offside A position from where you are not allowed to take part in the game, generally when you are in front of the ball when it is in your team's possession.

Overlap A situation during an attack by your team when you have more attackers to pass to than there are opposition defenders.

P

Pass When the ball is thrown or given from one player to another.

Penalty goal A goal scored from a penalty kick, worth 3 points.

Penalty kick A kick awarded to the non-offending team after an infringement.

Place kick A kick of the ball after it has been placed on the ground.

Possession When a team has control of the ball.

Prop Each team has two props, who wear numbers 1 and 3 and support the hooker during scrums.

Punt Kicking the ball after you have dropped it and before it hits the ground.

Put-in The act of throwing the ball into the scrum by the scrum-half.

R

Referee The official who controls the game and ensures that it is played according to the laws.

Reverse pass A pass that is thrown under your arm.

Rolling maul A maul where the ball-carrier, supported by one or more team-mates, starts to move forwards.

Ruck A situation where one or more players from each team, who are on their feet, close around the ball, which is on the ground between them.

S

Scrum A trial of strength in which the forwards of each team bind together and try to push the opposition away from the ball, which is put in between them.

Scrum-half The player who wears the number 9 and acts as the link between the forwards and the backs.

Set piece The term used to describe a scrum or line-out, both of which are formed, or set, by the referee before play restarts with a put-in or throw-in.

Sevens A version of rugby where each team has only seven players.

Side-step A sudden change of direction by the ball-carrier to avoid being tackled.

Swerve A sudden change in your running line from straight to around a defender.

T

Tackle Stopping a ball-carrier from making progress by wrapping your arms around the body or legs and bringing the opponent to the ground.

Throw-in When the hooker throws the ball into the line-out from the touchline.

Touchline The two lines down each side of the pitch that mark the playing area.

Touch judges The two officials who run along the touchlines to assist the referee.

Try A try is made by touching the ball down in the opponents' in-goal area. It is worth 5 points.

W

Winger Each team has two wingers, numbers 11 and 14, who attack or defend along the sides of the pitch.

Useful addresses

Here are the addresses of some major rugby associations that you may find useful.

International Rugby Board
Huguenot House
35-38 St. Stephen's Green
Dublin 2
Eire
www.irb.org

Rugby Football Union
Rugby Road
Twickenham
Middlesex TW1 1DZ
England
www.rfu.com

Irish Rugby Football Union
62 Lansdowne Road
Ballsbridge
Dublin 4
Eire
www.irfu.ie

Scottish Rugby Union
Murrayfield
Edinburgh EH12 5PJ
Scotland
www.sru.org.uk

Welsh Rugby Union
PO Box 22
Cardiff CF1 1JI
Wales
www.wru.co.uk

Australian Rugby Football Union
PO Box 188
North Sydney 2060
Australia
www.rugby.com.au

New Zealand Rugby Football Union
PO Box 2172
Wellington
New Zealand
www.nzrugby.co.nz

South African Rugby Football Union
PO Box 99
Newlands 7725
Cape Town
South Africa
www.sarfu.org.za

A rear tackle

Index

Acknowledgments

Dorling Kindersley would like to thank the following people
for their kind help in the production of the book:

Special thanks to Haslemere Junior Rugby Club for the use of their facilities and all the young rugby players for their skill and enthusiasm; Charles Adesarya, Chris Bird, Morgan Chandler, Thomas Chapman, Giles Chester, Charles Cooper, Nicholas Crompton, Tom Currie, Ben Eaton, Alex Foster, Jonathan Grill, Gary Howden, James Iacovou, Jonathan Kerridge-Smith, Mark Lambert, Alex Manos, Ben Morgan, Steven O'Neil, Robert Pudge, Charles Rawstron, James Reilly, Phillip Reith, Duncan Rogers, George Saunders, Ben Searle-Baker, Richard Sears, Jamie Simpson, Simon Taylor, Edward Thomas, Joshua Turner, James Wainwright, Blair Wood; King Edward's School; Chipstead Junior

Rugby Club for playing the match; Esme Fellows, James Noorani, Henry Stafford, Hannah Yate from Frensham Heights school; Peter Finneran, Tony Manos, Dave Rogers, and Bill Simpson for coaching; Malcolm Caird for refereeing; Rosellen Mates from Frensham Heights school; Linda McQuillan for looking after the kits; Ram Rugby for the balls and equipment; Mizuno for the boots; NEC Harlequins for the blue shirts; Halbro for the red shirts; Caroline Greene, Sue Leonard, Clare Lister, and Lee Simmons for editorial assistance; Angela Anderson for picture research; Hilary Bird for preparing the index; and Karen Lieberman for designing the jacket.

Picture credits
The publisher would like to thank the following for their kind permission to reproduce their photographs:
a=above, c=centre, b=below, l=left, r=right, t=top
Allsport: 4c, 4tl, Dave Rogers 5br, 25tl, 27t, 34t, 44cl, 43t, 43b, 45, Clive Brunskill 4bl, Jamie McDonald 42cl, Mike Hewitt 4br; **Mike Brett:** 25tr, 29b; **Colorsport:** 4cla, 8tr, 19br, 23tl, 35tr, 42t, 42b, 44b; **Mary Evans Picture Library:** 5c, 5crb; **Graham J Hedges:** 5tl; **Popperfoto:** Bob Thomas 44t; **Presse E Sports:** 5cl; **Topham Picturepoint:** 44cr. **Jacket: Colorsport:** tl.